SERIES TITLES

Antonella Pastorelli pp. 16–17; Luisa della Porta pp.30, 32–33; Paola Ravaglia pp. 15, 34–35;
Claudia Saraceni pp. 10–11; Sergio pp. 20–21
Smaller illustrations: Studio Stalio (Alessandro Cantucci, Fabiano Fabbrucci, Margherita Salvadori)
Maps: Paola Baldanzi
Photos: Corbis/Contrasto, Milan pp. 6–7b ©Adam Woolfitt; Scala Archives, Florence pp. cover, 22r, 24–25
Art Director: Marco Nardi
Layouts: Rebecca Milner
Project Editor: Loredana Agosta
Research: Loredana Agosta, Claire Moore, Ellie Smith
Repro: Litocolor, Florence

Consultant: Dr. SIMON JAMES, Senior Lecturer in Archeology at the School of Archeology & Ancient History, University of Leicester. Dr. James, former lecturer in prehistory and ancient Roman history for the British Museum, has participated in numerous excavations in Britain, France, Germany and Italy. He has also written several books on past cultures, for children and for adults, and continues to be involved in television documentaries as a script consultant.
A special thanks to art historian and archeologist Dr. JEANNINE DAVIS-KIMBALL, Center for the Study of Eurasian Nomads, for her insight on Sarmatian warrior women.

THE ROMAN WORLD
was created and produced by McRae Books Srl
Via del Salviatino, 1 — 50016 — Fiesole (Florence), (Italy)
info@mcraebooks.com
www.mcraebooks.com

Publishers: Anne McRae, Marco Nardi
Series Editor: Anne McRae
Author: Tony Allan
Main Illustrations: Emmanuelle Etienne pp. 12–13, 26–27; Giacinto Gaudenzi pp. 8, 28–29; Giacinto Gaudenzi and Francesca D'Ottavi 42–43; MM comunicazione (Manuela Cappon, Monica Favilli) pp. 18–19, 38–39; Alessandro Menchi pp. 36–37, 44–45;

Library of Congress Cataloging-in-Publication Data

Allan, Tony, 1946-
  The Roman world / Tony Allan.
      p. cm. -- (History of the world ; 4)
  Summary: "A detailed overview of the history of the Roman Empire, covering how it came to power in Europe and up to the fall of the Western Roman Empire in 476 CE"--Provided by publisher.
  Includes index.
  ISBN 978-8860981592
  1. Rome--History--Juvenile literature. 2. Rome--Civilization--Juvenile literature. 3. Civilization, Ancient--Juvenile literature. I. Title.
  DG77.A573 2009
  937--dc22
                                          2008008402
Printed and bound in Malaysia

The Roman World

Tony Allan

Consultant: Dr. Simon James, Senior Lecturer in Archeology at the
School of Archeology & Ancient History, University of Leicester.

Zak
BOOKS

Contents

The Celts were skillful metalworkers. This helmet, topped with a bronze hawk with flapping wings, would have been used for ceremonial purposes only.

Note—This book shows dates as related to the conventional beginning of our era, or the year 1, understood as the year of the birth of Jesus Christ. All events dating before this year are listed as BCE (Before Current Era). Events dating after the year 1 are defined as CE (Current Era).

TIMELINE

	9000 BCE	1000 BCE	800 BCE	600 BCE
NEOLITHIC EUROPE	The Ice Age comes to an end. Hunter-gatherers move into northern Europe. Farming reaches Europe from the Middle East.			
CELTS		Hallstatt Culture emerges north of the Alps. The Celts use iron to make tools and weapons.		Early Celtic princedoms in central Europe.
STEPPE PEOPLES		The Cimmerians, Iranian nomadic steppe people, occupy areas of present-day Russia.	Scythians, steppe horsemen, drive the Cimmerians from the Russian Steppes.	
ETRUSCANS		Villanovan Culture emerges in northern Italy.	Etruscan civilization develops on the Italian peninsula. Greeks establish colonies in the Mediterranean.	Etruscan monarchy is established.	Romans drive out Etruscan monarchs.
ROMANS		First archeological evidence of settlement at Rome.	Legendary date of the founding of Rome.	The Roman Republic begins.
GERMANIC PEOPLES				

Introduction

As farming made its way westward from Greece to the rest of Europe, permanent settlements began to appear across the continent. During the Metal Ages technological innovations affected settlement organization and ritual life, but also triggered drastic changes in the relations between different societies, giving a boost to trade and warfare. The most powerful society of early Europe was that of the Romans. Through their expansion, the Romans came into conflict with the Etruscans and Greeks on the Italian peninsula and other peoples of Europe, such as the Celts, the Germanic tribes, and the nomads from the steppes of eastern Europe and Asia. By the 2nd century CE the Romans had reached the height of their power, dominating most of Europe, North Africa, and the Middle East. When their empire became too large to manage it was divided. The Empire in the West, however, was too weak to withstand foreign attacks and fell in 476, as centers of power moved to northern Europe. The Roman Empire in the East, on the other hand, continued for almost another thousand years.

Steppe horseman, shown in a detail from a felt wallhanging found in a tomb in the Altai Mountains (in Russia).

400 BCE	200 BCE	1 CE	200 CE	400 CE

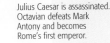

La Tène Culture starts replacing Hallstatt Culture.

Celts sack Rome.

The Mediterranean world comes into contact with the Scythians.

The Sarmatians, nomadic horsemen and warriors, conquer the Scythians.

The Etruscan city of Veii is conquered by the Romans after a ten-year siege.

Romans defeat the Celts settled in northern Italy.

Julius Caesar invades and conquers northern Gaul. Celts are Romanised.

Huns invade Germanic lands.

The Huns attack the Eastern Empire.

The Punic Wars begin.

Julius Caesar is assassinated. Octavian defeats Mark Antony and becomes Rome's first emperor.

The Empire is at its fullest extent during Emperor Trajan's reign.

The Roman Empire is divided.

Emperor Constantine makes Christianity official state religion. Emperor Theodosius I bans all pagan worship.

Collapse of the Roman Empire in the West.

The Germanic Cimbri tribe defeats Romans at Arausio.

The Romans occupy Germanic territory between the Rhine and Elbe rivers for a brief period.

Germanic forces destroy three Roman legions in the Teutoburg Forest.

The Germanic Alamanni tribe invades Italy.

Visigoths settle within the borders of the Roman Empire.

Vandals sack Rome.

Neolithic Europe

The Neolithic, or New Stone Age, was the time in which early Europeans stopped living as hunters and gathers and became farmers. Where they had once traveled constantly in search of game, they now settled down in villages. Regular harvests meant that there was more food to eat, and people had time to develop new skills, such as making pottery.

Horned oxen were the ancestors of today's cattle.

A reconstruction of Sesklo, a Neolithic faming village in Greece. Early villages were walled for defence against enemies and wild beasts.

Villages

Hunters had to keep on the move, often shifting camp to go in search of new herds to hunt and wild foods to gather. But farmers needed to stay put to tend the crops they had planted. So they started building permanent settlements—the first villages. In southern Europe they built huts of dried mud, roofing them with reeds or straw. In the colder, wetter northern lands, they used wood or else wattle and daub—a lattice of twigs plastered with clay.

The First Farmers

Farming spread gradually across Europe from the Middle East. The first farmers continued to hunt and gather wild food as their ancestors had done, but also started to plant crops as a sideline. In time they found the harvest was a more reliable source of food than wild game. The next step was to settle down on the lands they had planted.

Picks and digging sticks made from deers' antlers were used to turn soil.

Domestication of Animals

Besides growing crops, farmers learned to keep cattle, sheep, pigs, and goats. They chose gentle animals, driving away or killing the fiercer ones, so gradually tame breeds developed. The animals provided not just milk and meat but also wool and hides for making clothing.

Pottery pig from Turkey. Pigs were kept for meat.

Monument Builders

From about 4500 BCE on, people in western Europe started building large monuments made of earth or stone. Sometimes they put up standing stones called megaliths. Elsewhere they constructed burial chambers topped with flat stones that were originally covered with barrows. Some people built stone circles that were probably used for religious rituals; the best known is England's Stonehenge, which was begun as an earthen monument.

A rock painting showing people driving a herd of sheep into an enclosed area.

MEGALITHIC MONUMENTS

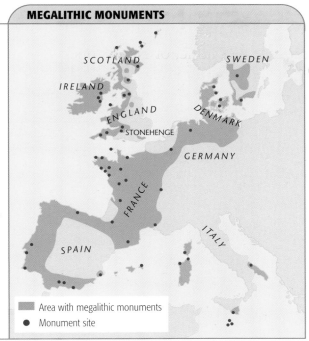

Standing Stones
Europe's megalithic monuments are concentrated in the western part of the continent. The upsurge in stone construction seems to have been linked to the spread of farming. It is still unclear, though, whether the monuments were put up by the farming peoples themselves or by the hunter-gatherers they were replacing. One theory is that they were constructed partly as a way of showing ownership of the land, discouraging newcomers from moving into an area.

SCOTLAND
IRELAND
ENGLAND
STONEHENGE
SWEDEN
DENMARK
GERMANY
FRANCE
ITALY
SPAIN

- Area with megalithic monuments
- ● Monument site

Crafts
It was not just chance that pottery came into use soon after farming began. Unlike hunters, farmers had permanent homes in which to house the new vessels, which they needed to store water and grain. Potters soon learned how to strengthen pots by firing them in the clay ovens used to bake bread.

A terra-cotta statuette from Romania.

The inner circle of standing stones at Stonehenge.

EARLY TRADE ROUTES IN EUROPE

ATLANTIC OCEAN

ENGLAND

FRANCE

SPAIN

Rhine

Rhône

Danube

Elbe

Po

Tiber

ITALY

CARPATHIAN BASIN

MEDITERRANEAN SEA

—— Atlantic
—— Rhine / Danube
—— Western Mediterranean
—— Eastern Mediterranean
—— Carpathian

The Bronze Age

For thousands of years early humans survived in Europe using tools made only of stone and wood. Then, from about 2500 BCE on, people started to turn to metals, first used in the Near East several centuries earlier. At first they used copper, but it was soft and easily blunted. Then they learned how to mix copper with tin to make bronze—a much harder metal.

A Bronze Age horned helmet from Zealand, Denmark.

In Search of Bronze

Since the production of bronze required both copper and tin, trade networks developed to supply the ores to regions that had one metal but not the other. Tin was especially hard to come by: the main sources were in western England and France, northern Italy, and northwest Spain. The traders who carried the ores also brought finished goods. Soon there was a flourishing luxury trade for bronze ornaments, weapons, and tools.

Metallurgy

To make bronze, metalsmiths had to melt copper over a high heat and then mix it with molten tin. Most bronze was made of about one part tin to nine parts copper. In Britain and France lead was also sometimes added, making the resulting metal easier to pour and to cast into the required shape.

While a village smith mixes bronze, other workers shape the hot metal into weapons and polish them ready for use.

Arms and Armor

Warriors wielding bronze swords and protected by metal body armor were more than a match for opponents who only had stone weapons. But bronze was scarce and expensive. The result was the development of warrior aristocracies who lorded it over the rest of society by force of arms.

This late Bronze Age cuirass, an upper body armor covering the chest and back, is from the Haute Marne region of France.

A relief showing a warrior and his arms—a lance, a sword, a flask, and a helmet at the top; a shield in the center; and part of a wagon at the bottom.

Burial

Archeologists investigating Bronze Age burial sites have noted a change in funerary customs from burying to cremating the dead. The new fashion started in eastern Europe in about 1400 BCE and spread across the continent over the following centuries. After cremation the ashes of the dead were buried in urns, so the culture associated with the change has become known as the Urnfield Culture.

Funerary urn with a chariot decoration dating back to c. 1300 BCE, found at a burial ground in Slovakia.

Found in Zealand in Denmark, the Trundholm Chariot is thought to represent a horse pulling the sun across the sky.

Salt Mines

One commodity that people could not do without was salt, which was used to preserve meat and fish, stopping them from going rotten. Salt mines in eastern Germany and Poland became important centers of trade, while mines at Hallstatt in Austria were to give their name to a whole culture of the ensuing Iron Age.

Cults and Beliefs

Little is known of Bronze Age religious beliefs, but archeologists have discovered that people in northern Europe threw objects including bronze ornaments and weapons into bogs as offerings to the gods. They also worshiped the Sun, to judge from the evidence of rock carvings and objects like the Trundholm Chariot (above).

Miner's pick axe and shovel of maple wood, discovered in the Hallstatt salt mines.

THE BRONZE AGE

c. 2500 BCE
Unetice Culture of central Europe is the first in Europe to make use of bronze.

c. 2300 BCE
Bronze casting reaches the Balkans, Greece and Italy.

c. 2000 BCE
Trade routes carry amber and metals across Europe.

c. 1800 BCE
Bronze working first appears in Britain.

c. 1650 BCE
Greece's Bronze Age Mycenaean civilization gets under way.

c. 1400 BCE
Walls are built around Mycenaean cities.

c. 1350 BCE
Urnfield Culture appears in central Europe.

c. 1250 BCE
Traditional date of Trojan War.

c. 1200 BCE
First iron objects appear in Europe.

c. 1200 BCE
Time of troubles, marked by large population movements, brings a dark age to the eastern Mediterranean.

c. 1000 BCE
Iron comes into widespread use in eastern Europe.

Hallstatt Culture

The Hallstatt Culture is named after Hallstatt in Austria, where archeologists in the 19th century found an Iron Age cemetery near ancient salt mines. It gave its name to the Celtic culture of the late Bronze Age and Iron Age, a time of hillforts and rich princely burials often featuring horse-riding equipment and iron swords. Foreign goods found in Hallstatt graves show that trade was widespread.

Iron sword with a bronze hilt decorated with a human figure, found in eastern France.

La Tène Culture

Named for an archeological site near Lake Neuchatel in Switzerland, La Tène Culture gradually replaced Hallstatt Culture from about 450 BCE on. Metalwork became more elaborate from this date, perhaps because Celtic smiths had become aware of the magnificent products of Etruscan Italy to the south (see pages 14–17).

Iron Age Peoples

Bronze had made people's lives easier, but it was expensive and hard to obtain. From about 1000 BCE on, a new metal that was comparatively cheap and plentiful began to spread across Europe. This was iron, and knowledge of its use was carried by Celtic metalsmiths. Iron did not need to be mixed in an alloy as bronze did, and there were deposits on hand in many lands. It could be used to make arms that were sharper and tougher than ones made of bronze. In the Bronze Age only rich warlords could afford swords and spears; now whole tribes could be armed with the new weapons.

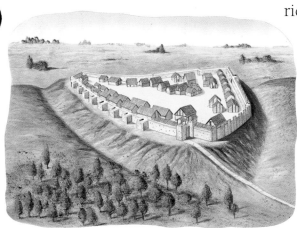

For security, Celtic peoples across Europe built hillforts that could be defended against raiders.

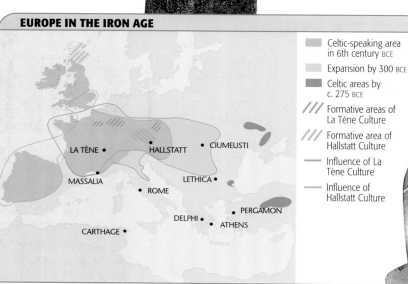

EUROPE IN THE IRON AGE

- Celtic-speaking area in 6th century BCE
- Expansion by 300 BCE
- Celtic areas by c. 275 BCE
- /// Formative areas of La Tène Culture
- /// Formative area of Hallstatt Culture
- Influence of La Tène Culture
- Influence of Hallstatt Culture

LA TÈNE •   HALLSTATT •   • CIUMEUSTI

MASSALIA •   LETHICA •

• ROME

• PERGAMON

DELPHI •   • ATHENS

CARTHAGE •

La Tène Culture bronze wine flagon with enamel and coral decorations.

The Celts in Europe

There was never a Celtic empire in Europe, because the Celtic peoples were not united. Instead they lived in different groups, each with similar habits and beliefs and speaking similar languages—forerunners of modern Welsh, Gaelic, and Breton. The first traces of Celtic occupation have been dated back to 1200 BCE, but it was only after 800 BCE that they spread out widely on the European continent.

A carving possibly representing a Celtic deity.

Horse and Chariot

Celtic war chariots were the first to have metal-rimmed wheels. Metalsmiths learned to make the metal rims slightly smaller than the wooden wheels, then heated them so that they expanded before fitting them into place. As the metal cooled the rims shrank, fitting snugly into position.

Celtic warriors rode into battle on two-horse war chariots like this one. Side screens prevented the rider from getting caught in the wheels.

Burials

Iron Age Celts buried their dead with goods that they thought would be useful to them in the afterlife. Thinking that life after death would be much like life before it, they provided them with pots, bowls, and cooking utensils as well as jewelry, tools, and clothing. Chiefs and princes were sometimes buried under large earth mounds in richly-furnished burial chambers.

CELTS IN EUROPE

c. 1200–800 BCE
Late Bronze Age; early phase of Hallstatt culture.

c. 800–600 BCE
Early Iron Age Hallstatt Culture gets under way. The first Celtic hillforts are built. Richly-furnished burial chambers appear.

c. 600–475 BCE
Last phase of Hallstatt culture.

c. 600 BCE
Celts begin trading with Greeks at Massalia.

c. 550 BCE
Hallstatt Culture reaches Britain and Ireland.

c. 410 BCE
Celts from northern Europe cross the Alps into northern Italy..

Inside a Celtic burial mound. A chief's body was laid out on a bronze couch amid rich burial goods.

Chiefs and Tribesmen

The steppe peoples lived in warrior societies led by chiefs who guided the horsemen into battle. Tombs preserved by the frost of the Altai Mountains have shown that chiefs and powerful men and women lived in luxury and were buried surrounded by rich grave goods.

Griffin's head of gilded wood and leather dating back to the 5th century BCE, found in a tomb in the Altai Mountains of eastern Russia.

This 1st-century BCE silver medallion showing a yak standing among trees was found in a grave at Noin Ula, in eastern Russia.

Nomadic Steppe Peoples

While people across most of Europe were settling down to farming, the inhabitants of the steppes of southern Russia were living a nomadic life herding animals. They traveled constantly with their horses, goats, sheep, and cattle in search of fresh grazing lands, spending their days in the saddle and their nights in tents. People following a similar way of life lived all across the flat lands of Europe and Asia as far as the Chinese border.

MIGRATIONS OF THE STEPPE PEOPLES

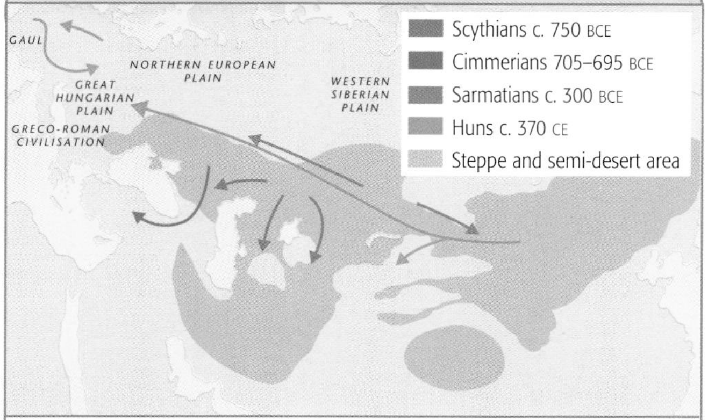
Scythians c. 750 BCE
Cimmerians 705–695 BCE
Sarmatians c. 300 BCE
Huns c. 370 CE
Steppe and semi-desert area
GAUL
NORTHERN EUROPEAN PLAIN
GREAT HUNGARIAN PLAIN
WESTERN SIBERIAN PLAIN
GRECO-ROMAN CIVILISATION

Horsemen from the East

The steppe horsemen inhabited a huge band of mostly flat land stretching from the Great Wall of China in the east to the Danube River in Europe—a distance of over 4,350 miles (7,000 km). The Scythians of eastern Europe shared the same culture and lifestyle as tribes whose graves have been excavated in the Altai Mountains of eastern Russia more than 2,500 miles (4,000 km) away, and may in fact have originally come from that region.

The Sarmatians

Between the 6th and 4th century BCE another nomadic people, the Sarmatians, made their way to the Ural Mountains from Central Asia. Like the Scythians, the Sarmatians were accomplished horsemen and warriors. They eventually conquered the Scythians and by the 2nd century BCE controlled most of southern Russia. During the 1st century CE the Sarmatians were strong enough to cause trouble even for the powerful Romans. The decline of the Sarmatians began with their defeat by the Goths in the 3rd century. They were finally crushed by the Huns (see page 45) in the late 4th century.

A golden comb found in the Ukraine. The decorative crest shows a horseman about to finish off a fallen enemy.

The Scythians

The ancient Greeks came into contact with steppe horsemen living in the lands north of the Black Sea. They called them Scythians. The Greek historian Herodotus (484? – 430? BCE) visited them and wrote of their warlike customs. He claimed they often scalped their enemies and used their skulls for drinking vessels.

Scythian Art

Despite their wandering lifestyles, Scythian craftspeople became skilled artists, working in gold, bronze, wood, and textiles. They developed a distinctive style featuring stylized real and imaginary animals. They mostly produced practical objects—tools, weapons, harnesses—that could easily be carried on horseback.

An electrum (gold and silver alloy) vase, made by a Greek craftsman for a Scythian nobleman in the 4th century BCE shows a man pulling out a tooth.

Unmarried Sarmatian women were skilled hunters and warriors who rode alongside men in battle. According to Herodotus, no Sarmatian girl could marry unless she killed an enemy in battle.

The Italian Peninsula

Iron Age Italy was divided up between many peoples. Most were farmers living in villages, but two groups had towns and a rich culture. In the north were the Etruscans, who grew rich through mining and trade. In the south, Greek settlers founded cities on the shores of mainland Italy and Sicily, bringing with them the knowledge of writing.

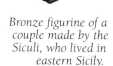

Bronze figurine of a couple made by the Siculi, who lived in eastern Sicily.

Some early Italians lived in houses of thatch built on piles over lakes.

A Diversity of Peoples

The early inhabitants of the Italian peninsula formed a patchwork of peoples of different races, languages, and cultures. Most lived in small villages or isolated farmsteads and supported themselves by farming and keeping livestock. Like Iron Age peoples in the rest of Europe, many built fortified settlements on high ground that could be easily defended against attack.

Contacts in the Mediterranean

Early Italian peoples had contact by sea with two great civilizations: the Greeks of the Aegean and the Carthaginians of the North African coast. Both founded settlements in Italy—the Carthaginians in western Sicily, and the Greeks in eastern Sicily and on the mainland. Both groups traded with their neighbors and also maintained close trade links with the Etruscans, who even learned the use of the alphabet from the Greeks.

This krater, found in the Etruscan city of Caere (modern-day Cerveteri), was made by a Greek artist in the mid-7th century. It shows a battle at sea.

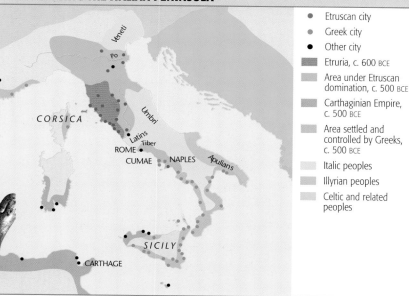

POPULATING THE ITALIAN PENINSULA

- ● Etruscan city
- ● Greek city
- ● Other city
- Etruria, c. 600 BCE
- Area under Etruscan domination, c. 500 BCE
- Carthaginian Empire, c. 500 BCE
- Area settled and controlled by Greeks, c. 500 BCE
- Italic peoples
- Illyrian peoples
- Celtic and related peoples

Veneti
Po
CORSICA
Umbri
Latins
Tiber
ROME
CUMAE
NAPLES
Apulians
SICILY
CARTHAGE

Peoples of the Italian Peninsula

Many of the peoples who lived in Italy before Roman times left little behind except for the names of regions: the Umbri in Umbria, the Apulians in the south-eastern region of Apulia, and the Veneti where Venice now lies. The Latin people lived in the area south of Rome. Celts invaded northern Italy in 410 BCE and established themselves in the lands north of the Po River. Greeks controlled much of the south coast.

The Etruscans

The Etruscans had the most advanced culture in Italy before Roman times. Their homeland, Etruria, occupied present-day Tuscany and reached down to the Tiber River in the south. By the 6th century their territory stretched further south and also included the Po Valley in the north and part of Corsica. Yet much about them remains mysterious. Scholars still argue over their origins; some claim that the Etruscans migrated to the Italian peninsula from Asia.

This detail of an Etruscan urn, which was used to store ashes of a cremated body, is decorated with a carving showing a banquet scene.

A 6th-century BCE Etruscan sarcophagus, bearing terracotta images of a dead couple from Caere.

Etruscan Practices

When Romans consulted soothsayers for advice about the future, they often used Etruscan techniques of divination. Etruscan diviners claimed to be able to discover the will of the gods by examining the livers of animals that had been sacrificed to them. Other methods included studying prodigies—unusual events like the birth of a two-headed calf—or watching out for flashes of lightning in the sky.

While citizens look on, an Etruscan soothsayer examines a sheep's liver for special marks, lumps, or discoloration that might help him discover the will of the gods.

Bronze model of a sheep's liver, used as a guide for Etruscan diviners.

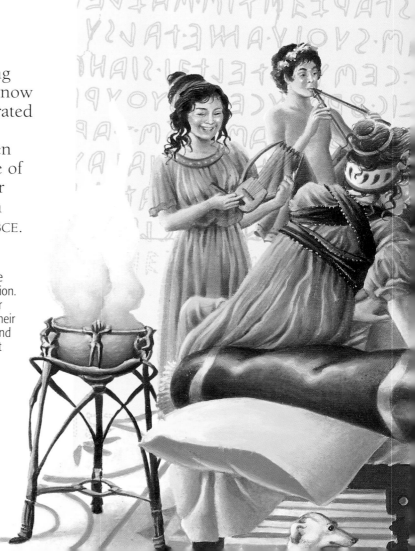

Iron Age Prosperity

The Etruscans built their prosperity on mining and working metals. There was iron ore on the Tuscan island of Elba, and iron and copper on the mainland. They used wealth from mining to build cities and produce fine art. Etruscan metalsmiths became famed abroad for their skills; one Greek observer noted that "their bronzes of every sort are the best for the decoration and service of homes."

A bronze chimera—a mythical beast part lion, part goat, with a tail in the form of a snake— skillfully crafted by Etruscan metalsmiths in the 4th century BCE.

Etruscan Culture

The Etruscans were a wealthy and advanced people who heavily influenced the Romans, handing down their religious beliefs, building technology, and artistic skills. Most of what we know about the Etruscans comes from brilliantly-decorated tombs excavated by archeologists over the past 250 years. Vivid wall paintings show wealthy men and women feasting, dancing, and enjoying a life of leisure. The Etruscans dominated central Italy for about 300 years until they were finally overtaken by the rising power of Rome in the 6th century BCE.

Art and Music

Tomb wall paintings provide vivid evidence of the Etruscans' love of color and decoration. Foreign observers also noted their taste for music, saying that they liked to go about their everyday business to the sound of pipes and lyres. One Roman writer even claimed that they used pipes to lure wild animals from their lairs when out hunting.

Detail of a late 5th-century BCE wall painting of a musician playing a double flute from Tarquinii (present-day Tarquinia), an Etruscan stronghold.

Traders went to sea in fully-rigged sailing boats with large cargo holds.

Language

The Etruscan language remains a mystery. It is unlike any other common tongue, and its only close relative seems to have been used in early times on the Greek island of Lemnos. Although about 10,000 inscriptions remain, they have never been fully deciphered, even though scholars can make out individual words and phrases.

Background: An example of Etruscan writing inscribed on an early 2nd-century BCE bronze tablet.

Etruscan merchants used gold and silver coins, mostly decorated on only one face.

Trade

Etruscan merchants traded goods all around the western Mediterranean. Besides metals, there was a flourishing trade in wine, carried in large pottery containers. From the 7th century on traders also exported Etruscan artworks, notably black pottery called *bucchero* ware that found its way to France, Spain, North Africa, and Greece.

Luxury-loving Etruscans enjoyed feasting to the sound of music while stretched out on couches.

Religious Beliefs

The Roman historian Livy (c. 59–17 CE) wrote that "the Etruscans are more devoted to religion than any other people." They believed in many gods, paying particular attention to the sky, which they divided into 16 regions, each ruled by a different deity. The care that wealthy Etruscans spent in preparing their tombs, which were decorated and furnished like second homes, show that they believed in an afterlife in which people continued to enjoy worldly pleasures.

Etruscan terra-cotta statue of the Greek god Apollo, known as the Apollo of Veii.

The Origins of Rome

Rome started out as just one of dozens of small, fortified settlements along the length of the Italian peninsula. Although it had grown to be a city by 600 BCE, it fell under the control of the Etruscans, its powerful northern neighbors. For about a century it was ruled by a line of Etruscan kings. Eventually the Romans rebelled, throwing out the kings and establishing a republic in their place.

The Foundation Myth
According to legend, Rome was founded by Romulus in 753 BCE. Romulus and his twin Remus were abandoned babies who were found by a nurturing she-wolf on Palatine Hill. Later they fell out; Romulus killed Remus in a dispute over the future of the city.

Detail of an Etruscan bronze statue of the legendary she-wolf.

EARLY ROME

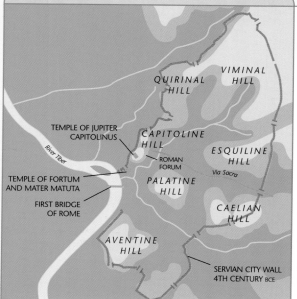

TEMPLE OF JUPITER CAPITOLINUS

QUIRINAL HILL

VIMINAL HILL

CAPITOLINE HILL

River Tiber

ROMAN FORUM

ESQUILINE HILL

Via Sacra

TEMPLE OF FORTUM AND MATER MATUTA

PALATINE HILL

FIRST BRIDGE OF ROME

CAELIAN HILL

AVENTINE HILL

SERVIAN CITY WALL 4TH CENTURY BCE

The Seven Hills
Like many Iron Age settlements across Europe, Rome was originally built on a hilltop for protection, and also to avoid the marshy ground around the nearby Tiber River. The Palatine Hill, where it began, was in fact one of a group of seven hills which would all eventually be occupied. As the city grew, houses were also built in the boggy valleys that lay between the hills. In time the marshes were drained, and the great city of Rome spread out on both banks of the river.

Early Inhabitants
Rome's first inhabitants were Latin-speakers related to other peoples who lived in the region of Latium, on the west coast of central Italy. The Palatine was the first of Rome's seven hills to be settled, in about 1000 BCE. Over the next two centuries villages were built on the neighboring hills. Rome grew into a powerful city-state and gradually came to dominate all the other surrounding city-states, some by conquest and others by alliance. Mastery of Latium was the first step in the process that saw Rome go on to rule much of the known world.

This 5th-century BCE stela bears the earliest known Latin inscription.

Bronze statuette of an Etruscan warrior.

The Etruscan Monarchy

In about 600 BCE, Rome and all of Latium came under the rule of a line of Etruscan kings. The last Etruscan dynasty, the Tarquin dynasty, is credited with the institution of Roman games (chariot races and gladiatorial fights) and the building of great public structures such as the Roman city walls, aqueducts, and temples.

Rome's first settlers were sheep-herders who built a village of thatched mud huts on Palatine Hill.

Rebellion

Although the Etruscans contributed much to Rome, their kings eventually became hated as tyrants. In 509 BCE the Romans rebelled against the Etruscans who had already been weakened by attacks from Celts and other rivals. The last Etruscan king, Tarquinius Superbus (reigned 534–509 BCE) was forced into exile. Rome became a republic, governed by a law-making Senate and two elected consuls, who took the place of the kings, holding office for only a year at a time (see page 21).

Bronze bust of Lucius Junius Brutus (active late 6th century BCE), legendary founder of the Republic. Brutus played a leading role in overthrowing the Etruscan monarchy.

THE RISE OF ROME

c. 1000 BCE
First archaeological evidence of settlement at Rome.

753 BCE
Traditional date for the foundation of Rome.

c. 600 BCE
The Etruscan monarchy is established.

509 BCE
The last Etruscan king is expelled from Rome. The Republic begins.

496 BCE
Romans defeat Latins at Lake Regillus.

396 BCE
Rome conquers its Etruscan neighbor Veii after a ten-year siege.

338 BCE
Rome completes the conquest of Latium.

Romanisation

Rome spread its power by offering Roman citizenship to many of the peoples it conquered, giving them the same rights as the Romans themselves—a process called Romanisation. When the Romans overcame their former Etruscan masters they extended citizenship rights to them. The Etruscans ended up being absorbed by Rome and losing their own identity.

Etruscan model of the Temple of Vulci. The Romans copied Etruscan designs for their own temples.

The Roman Republic

Republican Rome lasted for almost 500 years, a time that saw Rome grow from a small city-state to the dominant power in the Mediterranean world. In these years Rome was constantly at war – first with its Italian neighbors, then with Carthage, Greece and Celtic Gaul. At home, republican government broke down in the 1st century BCE into dictatorship and civil war.

Roman politicians had their names written on city walls during election time as part of their campaigning.

Patricians and Plebeians

When Rome became a republic, its government passed to its aristocrats, the patricians. The rest of the population—the plebeians—resented their powers. In the struggle of the orders that followed, the plebeians soon won concessions—first officials called tribunes to represent their interests, then a People's Assembly.

Politicians exchange views as a speaker addresses the Senate, Rome's chief law-making assembly.

The Punic Wars

Rome's chief rivals for control of the Mediterranean were the Carthaginians of North Africa (called *Punici* in Latin). Carthage was a great trading power whose interests inevitably clashed with Rome's when Rome began to expand overseas. The two powers fought three wars between 264 and 146 BCE. At the end of the third, the city of Carthage was razed to the ground.

CONTROL OF THE MEDITERRANEAN C. 500–201 BCE

MEDIOLANUM
AGNILEIA
ARAUSIO
GENUA
ARIMINUM
ANCONA
CASTRUM NOVUM
TARRACO
COSA
OSTIA • ROME
SAGUNTUM
NEAPOLIS
GADES
MALACA • CARTHAGO NOVA
TINGIS
RUSSADDIR
UTICA
CARTHAGE
HIPPO REGIUS
ZAMA
HADRUMETUM
LEPTIS MAGNA

A war elephant as used by the Carthaginians, shown on a 3rd-century BCE plate from southern Italy.

- ◼ Roman territory c. 500 BCE
- ◼ Roman territory by 290 BCE
- ◻ Roman territory by 272 BCE
- ◻ Roman territory by 218 BCE
- ◼ Roman territory by 201 BCE
- — Carthaginian territory c. 264 BCE
- ◻ Carthaginian territory c. 218 BCE
- ◼ Carthaginian territory c. 201 BCE

Victories in the Punic Wars

The First Punic War (264–241 BCE) was fought largely at sea, and ended with Rome taking control of Sicily. In the Second Punic War (218–201 BCE), the Romans gained control of southern Iberia, forcing out the Carthaginians. Eventually, Roman forces also invaded Carthaginian territory in Africa and defeated Hannibal at Zama. After the brief third war (149–146 BCE), the Romans gained control over the western Mediterranean.

The Senate

The Senate was the body that proposed new laws for Rome and made vital decisions about war and peace. At first all its members were patricians, but plebeians who had held important offices soon won the right to a seat. The Senate usually met in a building called the *Curia* in the Roman Forum. The number of senators varied over the years from 300 to 900; votes were held to decide what action to take.

Julius Caesar

Julius Caesar (100–44 BCE) was one of Rome's greatest talents— an outstanding politician and general who also won fame as a writer. Having brought Celtic Gaul under Roman control, he fought a civil war against his rival Pompey (106–48 BCE) before establishing himself as dictator at Rome. But his rise attracted enemies, who feared his ambition. In 44 BCE he was assassinated as he went to address the Senate.

Crisis in the Republic

In the 1st century BCE constitutional government broke down as rival generals competed for power. First Caesar and Pompey fought a civil war that ended in victory for Caesar. When he was assassinated, his adopted son Octavian (63 BCE–14 CE) battled with Mark Antony (c. 83–30 BCE) for supreme power. Peace was restored only after Octavian's navy defeated Antony and his ally, Queen Cleopatra of Egypt (c. 70–30 BCE), at Actium in 31 BCE.

Portrait bust of Julius Caesar, conqueror of Gaul and dictator of Rome from 48–44 BCE.

Painting from the Golden House of Nero, built on land razed by the Great Fire of Rome of 64 CE (see page 41).

The Age of Emperors

Once Octavian, Julius Caesar's adoptive son, took power as the first emperor, Rome never returned to republican rule. For the first three centuries of the Empire—a period known as the Principate—the emperors continued to respect republican raditions, seeking the Senate's advice before taking action. Later that pretense was dropped and the emperors ruled supreme and alone.

Onyx cameo of an eagle, the emblem of imperial power. The bird holds a victor's laurel wreath in its claws.

The Emperor

The imperial title was kept in the family. For a time in the 2nd century CE—the age of the "five good emperors"—reigning emperors adopted suitable heirs. In the 3rd century emperors were mostly made and unmade by the legions. From 286 CE on, there were usually at least two emperors ruling at once, one in the East and one in the West (see page 42).

The title Augustus was conferred upon Octavian when he became emperor. This statue of Augustus (reigned 31 BCE–14 CE) shows him as a military leader. Scenes of victory decorate his ceremonial breastplate.

Coin bearing a portrait of Emperor Hadrian. The emperor's face was everywhere in imperial Rome.

IMPERIAL RULE

27 BCE
Octavian conquers Egypt and assumes power as Emperor Augustus.

43 CE
Emperor Claudius' (reigned 41 BCE –54 CE) engineering projects improve water supply and alleviate food shortages.

80 CE
The Colosseum is completed under the Emperor Titus.

106 CE
Emperor Trajan conquers Dacia.

180 CE
Emperor Marcus Aurelius dies leaving behind his philosophical writings, The Meditations.

235 CE
Time of troubles begins: 31 emperors hold power over the next 50 years.

284 CE
Emperor Diocletian (reigned 284–305 CE) restores imperial authority.

286 CE
Emperor Maximian (reigned 286–305, 307–308 CE) is appointed co-emperor in the west by Emperor Diocletian.

313 CE
Emperor Constantine (reigned 307–337 CE) makes Christianity the state religion.

476 CE
The last Western emperor is deposed.

Imperial Residences

The Palatine Hill had a special significance for the Romans since the very beginning of their history (see page 18). Emperor Augustus was born and lived on the Palatine, and his successors went on to build luxurious residences which dominated the hill. The Palatine became the official residence of the Roman emperors. Some emperors, like Hadrian, (reigned 117–138 CE) also built other residences outside Rome.

Bronze equestrian statue of Emperor Marcus Aurelius (reigned 161–180 CE), last of the so-called "five good emperors" who gave Romans a period of stable government between 96 and 180 CE.

Julio-Claudian Dynasty

The problems of hereditary succession soon showed up in Rome's first dynasty, which ruled from 27 BCE. Emperor Augustus, its founder, was a brilliant leader, but two of his successors, Caligula (reigned 37–41 CE) and Nero (reigned 54–68 CE), were possibly mad. The dynasty ended in chaos and civil war in 69 CE, a year in which four men claimed the title of emperor: three of them met violent deaths.

Flavian Dynasty

This short-lived dynasty was founded by the soldier-emperor Vespasian (reigned 69–79 CE), who restored order after the disastrous year of 69 CE. The Flavians came from country gentry and owed their rise to the army. Emperor Vespasian himself and his son Emperor Titus (reigned 79–81 CE) were both successful generals, but the last Flavian, Emperor Domitian (reigned 81–96 CE), was a tyrant whose rule ended in a reign of terror. He was assassinated in 96 CE.

Bust of Emperor Caracalla, who granted Roman citizenship to all freeborn inhabitants of the empire in 212 CE.

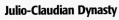
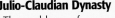

Emperor Hadrian's summer retreat, located near Tivoli, about 37 km (24 mi) northeast of Rome, was a huge complex with houses, baths, theaters, libraries, and hippodromes.

Severan Dynasty

The Severan Dynasty was founded in 193 CE by Emperor Septimius Severus (reigned 193–211 CE), an army leader who defeated three rivals to claim the throne. His successors all came to violent ends: one of his sons, Emperor Geta (reigned 211 CE), was killed on the orders of the other, Emperor Caracalla (reigned 211–217 CE), who himself was later assassinated. The last of the Severans, Emperor Alexander Severus (reigned 222–238 CE), was killed by his own soldiers.

Bust of Trajan (reigned 98–117 CE), the emperor who enlarged the empire to its greatest extent early in the 2nd century CE.

Education

Rome had no state schools. Children of the wealthy were taught at home by tutors or by self-employed schoolmasters. The school day started early, at dawn, and ended early in the afternoon. Students learned reading, writing, and arithmetic. At age 11, boys could go on to secondary schools to learn Latin and Greek literature and public speaking. Girls over 11 were usually taught at home.

Literature and the Arts

Rome owed a huge debt to Greece in the arts. In its early years it had few artistic traditions of its own, but the conquest of Greece in the 2nd century BCE brought it into contact with the greatest artworks of the ancient world. The result was a vogue for all things Greek that triggered a creative upsurge among the Romans themselves, especially in literature. Great Roman authors like Virgil and Ovid are still read today.

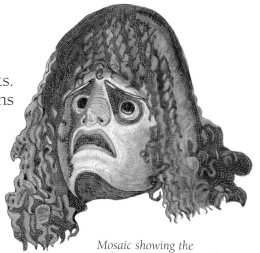

Mosaic showing the mask a tragic actor would have worn on stage.

Bust of Cicero, a leading politician and lawyer famed now for his writings.

Literature

The golden age of Latin literature lasted about a century, between 80 BCE and 17 CE. Cicero (106–43 BCE), Lucretius (active 1st century BCE), Catullus (c. 84–54 BCE), Virgil (70–19 BCE), Horace (65–8 BCE), and Ovid (43 BCE –17 CE) are some of the greatest names of the period. Every schoolchild knew Virgil's *Aeneid*, Rome's national epic, telling the story of how the Romans first came to the Italian peninsula.

Mosaic from North Africa showing the poet Virgil seated between the muses of history and tragedy.

The Theater

Rome only got its first permanent theater in 55 BCE, but the art form was soon well-established. The actors were slaves or freedmen, and men played women's parts. In the early days, the actors wore masks—sad for tragedy, caricatured for comedy. Mime shows were popular.

Mosaic from Pompeii showing a scene from a comic play featuring musicians.

A Roman copy of the original bronze sculpture Doryphours, or "spear-bearer," by the Greek artist Polyclitus (active 5th century BCE).

Artists of the Roman era mastered the art of portraiture. This portrait of a boy from Egypt was painted on a piece of wood which was placed over the face of his mummy.

Mosaics

Works of art called mosaics, made up of tiny brightly-colored stones known as *tesserae*, imitated paintings, achieving both abstract and representational effects. Because the stones were hard-wearing, mosaics were often used to decorate floors.

DECORATED INTERIORS

Most of the surviving paintings of the Roman era come from the towns in the Bay of Naples which were buried, and consequently preserved, by the eruption of Mount Vesuvius in 79 CE. Works from the towns of Pompeii and Herculaneum reveal the Romans' love for bold colors and fantastic decoration. Whole rooms were decorated; some with paintings giving the illusion of three-dimensional space. The most common subjects were nature and mythological scenes. This 1st-century BCE wall painting below from the Villa of the Mysteries in Pompeii, shows rites of the Dionysiac mystery religion.

Sculpture

Rome literally brought a taste for sculpture back from the wars: thousands of Greek statues were carried off to Italy as booty. Romans never lost their taste for the Greek style in the centuries that followed, and there was a flourishing trade in copies, often made by Greek artists living in Italy.

Gaul

The Rhône Valley was occupied by Gaulish lords who controlled important trade routes in the area. In the 2nd century BCE the Romans were drawn to the area after their Greek ally, Massalia (present-day Marseilles), asked for help against the threatening Gauls. Roman forces consequently established military strongholds, marking the beginning of Roman dominance in Gaul.

Trading at a port on the River Rhône. Trade was controlled and taxed by Gaulish noblemen.

TRADE ROUTES

Area of Celtic settlement or area inhabited by Celtic speakers c. 500 BCE

→ Trade Route

BROIGHTER

VIX • HEUNEBURG

RIVER RHÔNE

LIGURIANS

ETRUSCANS

SPINA

MASSALIA

IBERIANS

ROME

HUELVA
CADIZ

ATHENS
CORINTH

CARTHAGE

Trade of Luxury Goods and Raw Materials
The Rhône Valley provided an early channel for trade with the Greek city-state of Massalia (Marseilles) near the river's mouth. The Celts provided leather, textiles, salted meat, and slaves—usually prisoners of war—in return for pottery, metalwork, and wine. After the Roman conquest, the entire Celtic world was criss-crossed by traders bringing goods from the empire's most distant lands.

Celtic Europe

By the 3rd century BCE Celtic territory reached its greatest extent, stretching from Spain and Ireland to parts of modern-day Turkey. Though the Celtics worshiped similar gods and spoke related languages, they never came together to form one nation. Their loyalties were to the tribe, and different tribes were often at war. Ultimately, this led to their decline and Celtic tribes fell to Roman forces. Many tribes however maintained their identity under Roman rule.

The boar, Celtic symbol of power and strength, was considered a sacred animal. This 4th-century BCE bronze boar was found in France.

Celtic Language

The various Celtic languages all descended from a single tongue, referred to as Common Celtic. As the tribes split apart, different languages appeared. A marked division grew up between the Celtic spoken in Britain and Ireland and that in continental Europe. Celts in Gaul learned to use Greek letters to write down census records.

This tubular gold torque, an ornament worn around the neck, was found in Ireland and dates back to c. 100 BCE.

Celtic inscription carved on a 2nd-century BCE stone tablet from Italy. Celtic language was used in Italy as early as the 6th century BCE.

Celtic Society

The Celtic hillforts of the Iron Age developed in later times into fortified settlements the Romans called *oppida*. Here lived the tribal chiefs, elected for life by the nobles who formed the next social layer. Leading warriors and priests called Druids also ranked high. Below them were well-off farmers and artisans, with laborers, serfs, and slaves at the bottom of the heap.

Britain and Ireland

Before the Romans' arrival, Celtic-speaking people occupied most of Britain and Ireland. Western Scotland was inhabited by another group of non-Celtic people called Picts. Britain was a famed center of Druidism, the Celtic religion. After the conquest, Celtic languages survived in Wales and Scotland. Ireland was never conquered by the Romans.

A statue of a Gaulish warrior of the late 1st century BCE wearing an iron mail shirt, cloak and a torque around his neck.

This 3rd-century BCE golden brooch from Celtic Spain shows a fearless warrior confronting a lion.

Warrior Culture

Fighting was a way of life for the Celts. Neighboring tribes frequently raided one another's lands to steal cattle, and the raids easily escalated into open war. No quality was more highly regarded than bravery in battle, which was celebrated by bards in songs and poems. Chiefs fought in chariots, other ranks on foot, and leading warriors often challenged one another to single combat.

CELTIC RISE AND DECLINE

390 BCE
Celtic warriors sack Rome.

279 BCE
Celts attack Greece, before settling in Asia Minor (modern-day Turkey).

192 BCE
Romans defeat the Celts settled in northern Italy.

181 BCE
Romans conquer the Celts of Cisalpine Gaul.

118 BCE
Romans establish Narbo Martius, a colony in southern Gaul.

58 BCE
Julius Caesar invades and conquers northern Gaul.

55 BCE
Julius Caesar raids England, returning in 54 BCE.

52 BCE
Julius Caesar completes conquest of Gaul.

21 CE
Tiberius (reigned 14–37 CE) suppresses a rebellion in Gaul.

43 CE
The Romans conquer southern England.

Defeat by Rome

For all the Celts' courage in battle, their armies were at best loosely organized and in the long run proved no match for the highly disciplined Roman legions. Celtic disunity also played a part; the tribes never managed to come together in a single, combined army. As a result Gaul fell to the Romans by 52 BCE and much of Britain in the 1st century CE.

Invasions

The Romans first fought Germanic warriors in the late 1st century BCE, when the Cimbri invaded northern Italy. Julius Caesar tried to pin the tribes behind the Rhine River, but from time to time they broke out. From the 3rd century on, Rome was on the defensive. Eventually the barrier broke, and Goths, Franks and Saxons swept across western Europe (see pages 44–45).

Tombstone of a Roman legionary who served and died on Rome's Germanic frontier.

This iron spearhead, found on a sacred site on the Danish island of Funen, is decorated with a pattern of circular inlays of silver and brass.

Warring Neighbors

The Germanic peoples who confronted the Roman Empire across the Rhine River were made up of a confusing mosaic of tribes. The lands they inhabited stretched from Scandinavia through Germany itself into southern Russia. They lived by farming and herding, and were organized in clans that from time to time allied against the Romans.

Germanic tribesmen attack soldiers defending Rome's frontier on the Rhine River.

GERMANIC PEOPLES IN EUROPE

Tribal Migration

The Germanic lands had no natural frontiers to the east, where they bordered on the vast plains inhabited by the nomadic steppe peoples. Whenever there was a major population movement westward among these horsemen, it had a knock-on effect on the Germanic tribes, pressing them west and south toward the Roman Empire's borders. This tendency reached a climax in the 4th century CE, when Asiatic Huns swept into the German lands, fatally increasing the pressure on Rome.

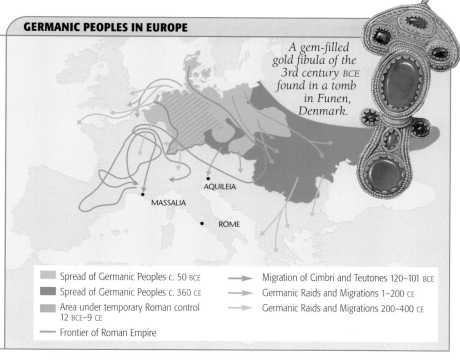

A gem-filled gold fibula of the 3rd century BCE found in a tomb in Funen, Denmark.

AQUILEIA

MASSALIA

ROME

Spread of Germanic Peoples c. 50 BCE	→ Migration of Cimbri and Teutones 120–101 BCE
Spread of Germanic Peoples c. 360 CE	→ Germanic Raids and Migrations 1–200 CE
Area under temporary Roman control 12 BCE–9 CE	→ Germanic Raids and Migrations 200–400 CE
Frontier of Roman Empire	

Rituals and Burials

The northern Germanic peoples worshiped the Norse gods Thor, Odin, and Freya. According to the Roman historian Tacitus (c. 56–120 CE), they performed rituals in the open air in forest groves. Archeologists have found the remains of people who died violent deaths thrown into bogs, perhaps as human sacrifices.

Body of a man found in Tollund Fen, Denmark. He had been strangled, perhaps as a sacrifice.

Decorated cup from a tomb uncovered in Denmark. The decorative motifs imitate the Roman style.

The Germanic Style

While the Germanic peoples imported many luxury goods, their craftsmen had a long tradition of their own, working mainly in wood and metals. Germanic taste tended to intricate patterns.

Trade

There was an active trade in metals and amber across the Germanic lands from Bronze Age times. During the Roman era, the flow of goods increased, particularly in border areas along the Rhine and Danube rivers. Clan chiefs gradually developed a taste for luxury goods, including Roman gold and silverware. By the time of the great invasions, the tribes were at least partly Romanised.

Roman cup from a Danish tomb. Trade carried luxury goods around Europe.

GERMANIC PEOPLES

105 BCE
Germanic Cimbri defeat Romans at Arausio.

58 BCE
Julius Caesar defeats the Suebi, setting Rhine River as Rome's frontier.

12–9 BCE
Roman general Drusus Germanicus (38–9 BCE) occupies German territory between the Rhine and Elbe rivers.

4 CE
The future Emperor Tiberius (reigned 14–37 CE) launches a fresh campaign.

9 CE
Germanic leader Hermann (d. 21 CE) destroys three Roman legions in the Teutoburg Forest.

16 CE
Emperor Tiberius recalls his general Germanicus Caesar (15 BCE–19 CE), bringing Germanic wars to a temporary end.

98 CE
Roman historian Tacitus writes Germania, a treatise on the origins of the Germanic tribes.

177 CE
Marcomanni invade across River Danube, to be driven back by Emperor Marcus Aurelius.

254–256 CE
Emperor Gallienus' (reigned 253–268 CE) victories over the Germanic peoples are commemorated on coins.

269 CE
The Alamanni invade Italy.

277–278 CE
Emperor Probus (reigned 276–282) restores the frontier on Rhine and Upper Danube.

Hadrian's Wall

When Emperor Hadrian decided that the empire should expand no further, he settled on a line roughly equivalent to the modern border between England and Scotland at its northern limit. To keep in check the northern tribes, which had never been fully conquered, he ordered the building of a wall that stretched along the frontier from sea to sea. Hadrian's Wall served for border control rather than as an impenetrable barrier. It remained in use to the end of the Roman occupation of Britain.

The Roman Empire

The Roman Empire was built up over many centuries. First Rome conquered the Italian peninsula, then the western Mediterranean following victory over Carthage in the Punic Wars. The conquest of Greece and Asia Minor took place in the 2nd century BCE. The imperial age proper got under way when the Roman Republic gave way to the rule of the emperors, from the time of Emperor Augustus on. For a century after the death of Augustus the empire continued to grow, reaching its greatest extent under Emperor Trajan in the early 2nd century CE.

The Porta Nigra at Trier, an imperial city in present-day Germany.

Roman sentries on guard duty along the wall searched people and wagons for smuggled goods or concealed weapons.

THE EXTENT OF THE EMPIRE

Extent of the Roman Empire 117 CE
— Hadrian's Wall

BRITANNIA

GALLIA

HISPANIA

ITALIA
ROME •

DACIA

ASIA

MESOPOTAMIA

MAURETANIA

AFRICA

LIBYA

PALAESTINA

Roman Expansion

Stretching from the Scottish border in the north to the Sahara Desert in the south, and from the Atlantic Ocean to the Persian Gulf, the Roman Empire at its greatest extent early in the 2nd century CE was the largest the western world had ever seen. Its central focus was the Mediterranean Sea, but additional provinces were added to the north, south, and east in a never-ending quest to conquer as much as possible. In the long run the empire over-reached itself: the task of defending the long land borders proved more than Rome could manage.

A GROWING EMPIRE

12 BCE
The empire's frontier is extended north to the Danube River under the emperor Augustus.

6 CE
Judaea becomes a Roman province.

9 CE
Rome's attempt to conquer northern Germany ends in defeat at Teutoburg Forest.

42 CE
Mauretania becomes a Roman province, completing the Empire's grip on the Mediterranean coast.

43 CE
Emperor Claudius conquers England. Lycia, in southwest Asia Minor, becomes a province.

106 CE
Arabia is annexed. The empire is at its fullest extent under the emperor Trajan.

113 CE
Armenia is conquered.

116 CE
Emperor Trajan conquers Mesopotamia.

The Provinces

An important cultural divide separated the empire's eastern and western provinces. The eastern part of the empire was Greek-speaking and made up of regions with a long history of urban civilization. In contrast, western provinces like Gaul and Britain were formed in what the Romans considered "barbarian" lands, with no previous tradition of city living. The split lay at the root of the empire's eventual division into eastern and western halves (see page 42).

Stone relief showing tax payment from Neumagen, Germany.

Relief from Leptis Magna, in the North African province of Tripolitania (present-day Libya).

The Pax Romana

The Roman Empire was mostly created by force, but once peace had been established it brought real benefits to its subjects. Under the Pax Romana ("Roman peace"), which was guaranteed by the legions, people could travel throughout a war-free empire. The result was an upsurge in trade and general prosperity.

Relief of the goddess Roma, divine personification of the strength and benevolent power of the empire.

Paying Taxes

The provinces had to bear the costs of running the empire, which grew as the size of the army and the bureaucracy increased. Under the emperors the amount individuals paid was settled by regular censuses of people's property. From the 3rd century on, taxes became so high that they stifled business activity, seriously weakening the empire.

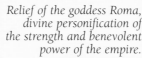

The Provincials

People in Rome's provinces benefited from mostly efficient administration and also from the long Roman peace, which allowed trade to flourish. Ambitious provincials could go to Rome to seek their fortune. From 212 CE on all freeborn adults shared the benefits of Roman citizenship. The main problem was taxation, which grew so heavy that it caused massive poverty and debt.

A woman pours perfume into a flask in this detail of a wall painting from a Roman house.

There were great cultural differences among the peoples in the Empire. This mosaic from Edessa (in the southeast of present-day Turkey) shows a family dressed in Syrian style. Their names are written in Syrian script.

Living in the Empire

Wealthy freeborn Roman citizens probably enjoyed a more comfortable lifestyle than anyone else in the ancient world. Well-off individuals lived in gracious villas and had the choice of buying any of a range of goods from all over the Mediterranean world. There were plays in the theaters to entertain them, and they enjoyed luxurious banquets at the homes of friends. Even the poor got free grain hand-outs if they lived in Rome itself. Yet there was also a downside to Roman life. Disease was widespread, affecting all classes. "Luxury diseases," such as gout, were common among upper-class males.

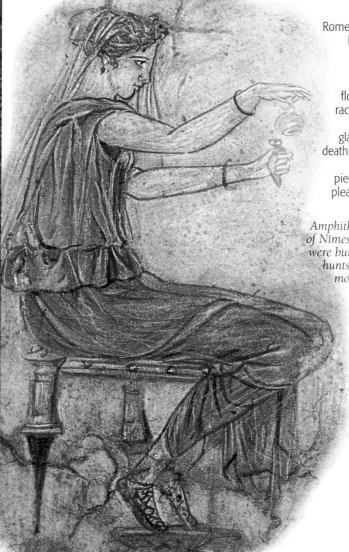

Entertainment

Rome's emperors sought to keep people happy by providing spectacular entertainments in the arenas. Huge crowds flocked to watch chariot races or else more brutal spectacles involving gladiators fighting to the death. Sometimes unarmed criminals were torn to pieces by wild animals to please the baying crowd.

Amphitheatres, like this one of Nîmes, in southern France, were built to host animal fights, hunts, gladiator fights and even mock naval battles when flooded.

Food

The main meal in ancient Roman times was supper, eaten around sunset. Wealthy Roman citizens ate more fish than meat, although pork was also popular. They had a wide range of vegetables, including cabbage, beans and lettuce. They also showed a taste for spicy sauces, particularly a strong-tasting fish sauce called *garum*. Snails and dormice were both bred for food.

A glass fruit bowl from a Roman fresco. Figs and grapes were the commonest fruits, but apples, pears and dates were also popular.

Men relax in the caldarium (warm-bath room) of a public baths. The heat was provided by a basement furnace.

Roman bathers used sponges and strigils–curved scrapers made of metal or bone–to wipe their bodies clean.

Daily Bath in Rome

Partly because their homes lacked running water, but mainly to meet friends, most Romans went to the public baths each day. Entrance fees were kept low so all free citizens could afford admission. Bathers could choose between cold- and warm-water pools, and some establishments also had vapor baths and sauna-like steam rooms.

Dress and Jewelry

At home, men and women usually wore loose, knee-length tunics. On public occasions they wore more formal, ankle-length togas (for men) and *pallas* (for women). Men regularly wore signet rings, but most jewelry was worn by women. Rich Roman ladies adorned themselves with gold and silver necklaces and bracelets and earrings studded with emeralds and pearls.

Gold belt buckle from the Thetford Treasure, found in England in 1979.

Back of a silver mirror from the House of Menander, Pompeii, dating back to the 1st century CE.

ROMAN GODS

Jupiter
Greatest and best of the gods, associated with the sky and with thunder and lightning.

Juno
Jupiter's wife. Goddess of marriage and childbirth.

Mars
God of war, also worshiped by farmers. The second most important of the Roman gods.

Venus
Partner of Mars, and goddess of love and beauty.

Janus
Two-faced god who guarded gates and doorways, and also new beginnings. The month of January is named after him.

Vulcan
God of fire, worshiped by blacksmiths.

Minerva
Goddess of wisdom; also a patroness of crafts and trades.

Mercury
The messenger of the gods, shown with hat, winged shoes and a staff with snakes entwined around it. Also the god of trade and merchants.

Vesta
Goddess of hearth and home, whose sacred fire was tended by the Vestal Virgins.

Saturn
God of agriculture and vegetation whose annual festival each December, the Saturnalia, was the Roman equivalent of Christmas.

Statue of the Emperor Claudius portrayed as the god Jupiter.

Religious Beliefs

The Romans believed in many different gods and goddesses. Some were their own—gods of agriculture and nature that their farming ancestors had worshiped. Others came from outside, from the Etruscans or the Greeks. There was an official state religion that involved sacrificing animals and repeating set ceremonies in the temples. It was every Roman's patriotic duty to follow these rites, but few found them spiritually satisfying. Instead they chose to worship their own household gods or else to follow foreign religions brought to Rome from the East.

The Imperial Cult

Roman gods acted like powerful humans, so in time it seemed natural to treat Rome's own greatest rulers as gods. Julius Caesar was the first Roman to be deified —pronounced a god after his death. Later, some of the best emperors were also declared gods by the Senate, but always after their death; while alive they were only human. All Romans were expected to worship the divine emperors.

Janus depicted on a coin. The cult of Janus was quite popular among the Romans.

A 1st-century BCE relief showing animals being brought to an altar for ritual sacrifice.

A lar, or household god, as shown in a detail from a 1st-century CE Pompeiian shrine.

Household Worship

For the Romans religion began at home. Each house had its hearth sacred to Vesta, and also its lares and penates. The lares were the spirits of dead ancestors, while the penates looked after the store cupboard, making sure the family had food to eat. Each day the head of the household would pray to the gods and would leave food offerings before the shrine where their images were kept.

Vestal Virgins tend the sacred flame at their temple in the Roman Forum. Romans believed that disaster would strike the state if the fire went out, and any Vestal who allowed it to happen was whipped.

The Vestal Virgins

Vesta was the Roman goddess of the hearth, and a fire burned in every home in her honor. The state decided that it too should have its own sacred flame, which burned in a temple in the Roman Forum in Vesta's honor. Four (later six) girls of noble birth were selected to guard it. They held the job for 30 years, during which they had to remain unmarried.

Christianity

Christianity reached Rome soon after the death of Jesus Christ. At first officials regarded it as just a troublesome sect, but as the faith spread, rulers feared that it was anti-Roman and launched major persecutions. Everything changed in the 4th century CE, when the Emperor Constantine became more tolerant of Christianity.

A Christian image of Jesus Christ portrayed as the good shepherd from the catacombs, underground burial places used by early Christians.

Foreign Religions

Christianity had rivals in the shape of other religions from the East. The first such cult to reach Rome was that of Cybele, the Great Mother, which came from Asia Minor. Then there was Mithraism, a Persian religion that was only open to men and was popular in the legions. In contrast, the worship of the Egyptian goddess Isis spread widely among women.

A sistrum, or rattle, used by priests of Isis in religious ceremonies and processions.

Altar of the Matronae Aufaniae, a triad of mother goddesses from Roman Germany.

Women's Work

The main job of freeborn women in ancient Rome was to run households. Girls were educated to be good housekeepers, although much of the domestic work was actually done by slaves. There were some women in the workforce, but they were mostly ex-slaves. If they could gather together some money, such freedwomen might become shopkeepers or innkeepers, or else get jobs as seamstresses, hairdressers, or nurses.

This stone shop sign from Ostia shows a woman selling fruit and poultry.

Detail from a mosaic showing a young household slave serving food.

Rome at Work

In Roman society most of the hard work was done by slaves. Rich Romans lived off the money that came to them as landlords or as owners of big estates—few jobs interested them except those in politics or the law. Even quite poor people often kept a slave or two to do the housework and the cooking. In time many slaves won their freedom, and these freedmen were happy to take jobs in shops and crafts that the Romans themselves avoided.

Slave Labor

From the 2nd century BCE on, Rome was a slave society on a huge scale; an estimated one-third of the population may have been slaves, and they did nearly all the work. Most slaves originally came to Italy as prisoners of war, although some were captured by pirates and sold through a famous slave market on the Greek island of Delos. Slaves were bought and sold like animals, and became their masters' property for life.

Life in the Army

Soldiering was a full-time profession in imperial Rome. Men signed up to serve in the legions for terms of 20 years, followed by five years in reserve in case of emergencies. Army service could take them to distant lands, anywhere from the Scottish border to the deserts of North Africa. At the end of their service they received retirement pay and sometimes a plot of land.

Soldiers wore iron helmets with neck protectors and plate armor covering their upper body.

Skilled Workers

The luxury trades that flourished in Rome provided jobs for goldsmiths, silversmiths, perfumers, and jewelers. There were artists and sculptors too, many of them born in Greek cities and specializing in copying Greek artworks, which became highly fashionable in Rome (see page 25). The Roman army also provided openings for skilled surveyors and engineers.

Surveyors used this instrument, called a groma, *to check levels and plot straight lines.*

Detail of a mosaic showing a baker taking a loaf of bread out of the oven. Bread was usually baked in the baker's shop.

Farming

In the early days, Rome was a nation of small-scale farmers. That changed when it became a conquering power. Increasingly, some parts of Italy were divided up into great estates worked by prisoners of war brought back to Rome as slaves. Even so, farming kept a special place in Roman hearts. Many a town-dweller's ambition was to escape from the city to farm a country smallholding.

Legionaries march out of a provincial town on a paved road, while slaves are busy at work in the countryside.

Roman Building Technology

BUILDING ACCOMPLISHMENTS

Concrete
First used in the 3rd century BCE. Made of sand from volcanic rocks mixed with lime, rubble, and water. Without it the great Roman monuments could not have been built.

Arches
Used to carry great weights and to build vaulted roofs and domes. Vaults and arches were supported by a timber framework that was removed when the concrete set.

Hoists
To lift heavy masonry, Roman engineers devised special hoists, powered by huge wheels turned by slaves. Pulleys operated by the wheel hauled heavy stone blocks high into the air.

Roads
Roman roads were built in layers on a base of levelled sand, topped with a foundation of large stones overlaid with pebbles and gravel. The top layer was made of cobbles or large paving stones or gravel set in concrete.

Basilicas
Long buildings with a central aisle flanked by columns separating off side aisles. The Romans used them for law courts and other official buildings, but the design was later copied for churches.

Triumphal Arches
Huge freestanding gateways covered in sculptures and inscriptions designed to celebrate military victories. A very Roman type of building. (See the arch of Constantine on page 43.)

Emperor Hadrian, a great builder who reconstructed the Pantheon in its present form.

R ome's genius was a practical one, and its civilization excelled in building roads, bridges, and aqueducts. If Greece was famous for her philosophers and poets, Rome's glory was her engineers. Using concrete—a Roman invention—they constructed towns and highways across the empire, many of which survive today. Their greatest triumph was the city of Rome itself, the center of the road network and the site of the empire's finest buildings.

Building an Empire
The empire provided great opportunities for building. The building of towns involved the construction of temples, public buildings, and defensive walls. Aqueducts were cut through the countryside to bring water for the citizens. Officials wanted out-of-town villas and retirement colonies were needed to house old soldiers.

An Impressive Water System
Engineers went to great lengths to bring fresh water to the cities. The water was carried underground where possible, but sometimes aqueducts had to be built to carry it over river valleys. Water carried over to towns by the aqueducts was piped to homes, baths and street fountains (see page 41).

Detail from Trajan's Column in Rome showing legionaries building a military camp.

Architects of Rome
The credit for the empire's great buildings went more to the emperors who ordered them than the architects who designed them. Few names of Roman architects have survived, although Vitruvius (active 1st century BCE), the author of a book on the subject, is still remembered. Many of the big construction projects were in fact carried out by engineers employed by the army.

The Pantheon
A temple to all the gods, the Pantheon was first built in 25 BCE but totally reconstructed under Emperor Hadrian. The main part of the building was a circular hall topped by the largest dome built in the ancient world. At its summit was a round hole that let in sunlight. The Pantheon became a church when the empire turned Christian, and is still standing today.

Cutaway diagram of the Pantheon, showing its revolutionary circular design and domed roof.

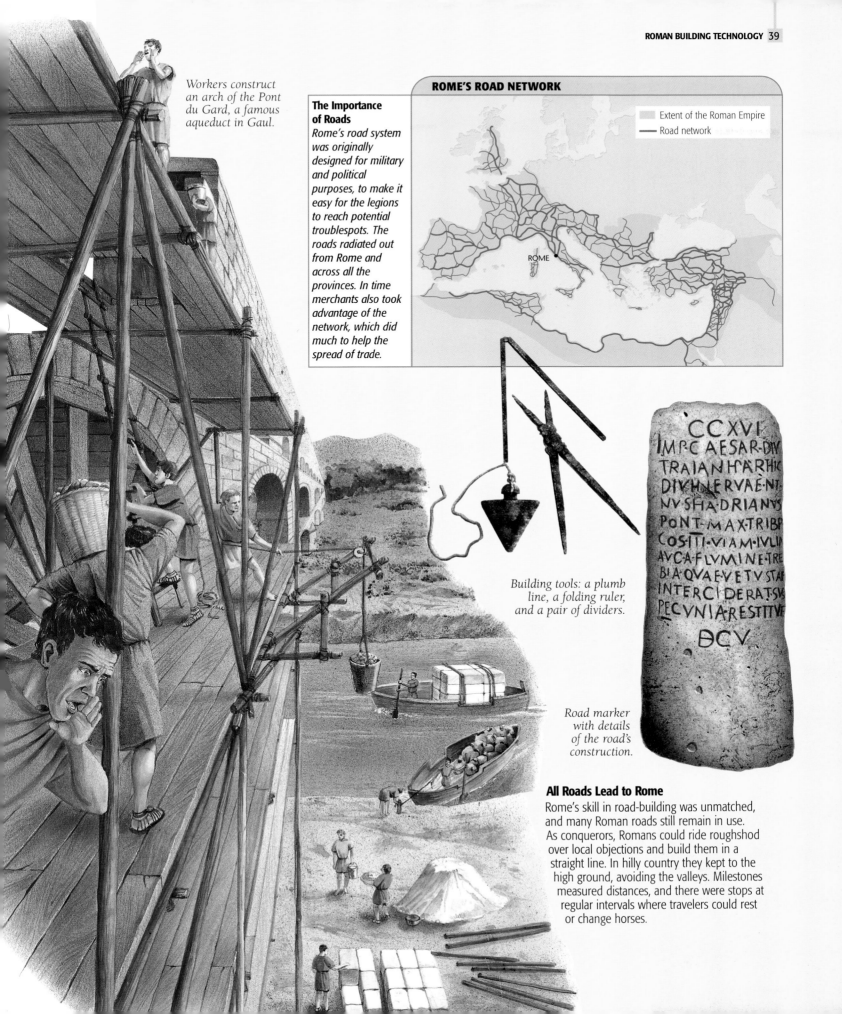

Workers construct an arch of the Pont du Gard, a famous aqueduct in Gaul.

The Importance of Roads

Rome's road system was originally designed for military and political purposes, to make it easy for the legions to reach potential troublespots. The roads radiated out from Rome and across all the provinces. In time merchants also took advantage of the network, which did much to help the spread of trade.

ROME'S ROAD NETWORK

Extent of the Roman Empire
— Road network

ROME

Building tools: a plumb line, a folding ruler, and a pair of dividers.

Road marker with details of the road's construction.

All Roads Lead to Rome

Rome's skill in road-building was unmatched, and many Roman roads still remain in use. As conquerors, Romans could ride roughshod over local objections and build them in a straight line. In hilly country they kept to the high ground, avoiding the valleys. Milestones measured distances, and there were stops at regular intervals where travelers could rest or change horses.

The City of Rome

The Rome of the emperors was the greatest city the world had ever known. More than a million people thronged its streets, which were adorned with fine monuments built with the wealth of conquered lands. Talented people from around the empire flocked to live there, and its citizens benefited from free bread and entertainments provided by the emperors to keep them happy. Yet there was another side to the city. The poorer districts were noisy and foul-smelling, crime was rife, and about a third of its inhabitants were slaves.

MONUMENTS OF ROME

1 Theater of Marcellus
2 Forum Holitorium (produce market)
3 Forum Boarium (cattle market)
4 Temple of Jupiter Capitolinus
5 Arch of Janus
6 Temple of Juno Moneta
7 Circus Maximus
8 Tabularium
9 Temple of the Divine Trajan
10 Temple of Concord
11 Arch of Septimius Severus
12 Basilica Julia
13 Forum of Trajan
14 Forum of Caesar
15 Curia
16 Basilica Aemilia
17 Temple of Castor and Pollux
18 Temple of Cybele
19 Markets of Trajan
20 Temple of Apollo
21 Forum of Augustus
22 Temple of the Divine Julius
23 Forum of Vespasian
24 Basilica of Maxentius
25 Imperial Palace
26 Domus Augustana
27 Domus Flavia
28 Temple of Venus and Rome
29 Temple of the Caesars
30 Palace of Septimius Severus
31 Septizonium
32 Aqua Claudia
33 Arch of Constantine
34 Colossus of Nero
35 Colosseum
36 School of the gladiators
37 Temple of the Divine Claudius
38 Aqua Marcia

The illustration below shows some of the major monuments of the city of Rome during the 4th century CE.

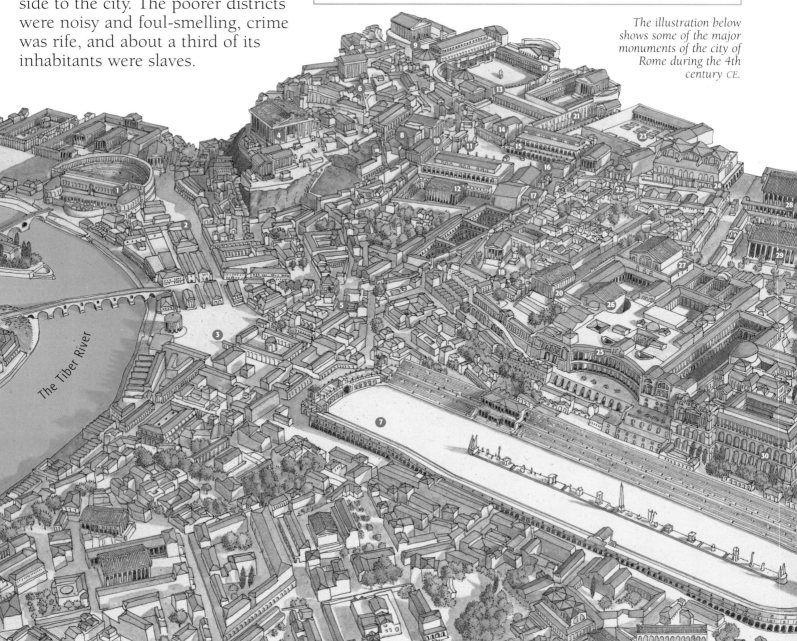

The Tiber River

Hazards in the City

Fire was a constant hazard in Rome's cheap and crowded tenements, which sometimes also collapsed because of their poor construction. In 64 CE, the Great Fire of Rome completely razed three of the city's 14 districts and partially destroyed seven more, leaving only four untouched. Other everyday hazards included being hit by litter thrown from upstairs windows.

Romans blamed Nero for starting the Great Fire of 64 CE to clear space for his palace.

Markets

The Roman Forum was the city's original shopping center, but by late republican times it was filled with public buildings, and the tradesmen, except for gold- and silversmiths, had moved on. New shopping areas were provided—the biggest, Trajan's Market, had room for 150 shops. The main fruit and vegetable markets were near the Tiber River. Shops also lined the streets; most consisted of a single room opening onto the road, with a flat above the premises where the shopkeeper lived.

Stone relief plaque showing a cloth merchant's shop, with fabrics and cushions hanging from a ceiling rack.

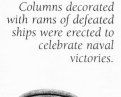

Columns decorated with rams of defeated ships were erected to celebrate naval victories.

The Forum

Most Roman towns had a central forum that served as a gathering-place and market. The Forum in Rome grew up in just such a way, but was later dignified with temples and public buildings, including the Curia where the Senate met. In imperial times different emperors added forums of their own to adjoin the original one.

Monuments to Victory

Rome's streets were full of monuments proudly celebrating military victories. The biggest were the triumphal arches (see page 38) built for the victory parades of emperors returning from battle. Tall sculpted columns were also popular—the best-known, Trajan's Column, rose 125 feet (38 m) high.

Water Supply

Rome's earliest aqueduct was completed in 312 BCE. By early imperial times there were eight of them, supplying about 47 gallons (180 liters) of water each day for every inhabitant of the city. Wealthy people had water piped to their homes, but the rest collected it from public fountains.

Stone fountains like this one were the main water source for ordinary Romans.

The Tetrarchy

When Emperor Diocletian decided to divide imperial authority, he took control of the Eastern lands and gave command of the West to an old friend, Maximian. Seven years later he extended the idea of joint rule by appointing two lesser co-emperors, Constantius I (reigned 305–306) and Galerius (reigned 305–311).The four-man system of government was known as the Tetrarchy, from a Greek word meaning "four."

Marble statue of Diocletian, Maxentius and the two lesser co-emperors, called Caesars.

The Late Empire

In the 3rd century CE the empire's problems multiplied. A strong new enemy arose in the East in the shape of Sassanian Persia; in 260, Persian forces defeated and captured the Emperor Valerian (reigned 253–260). Many other emperors came and went, some murdered by their own men. Inflation soared as spending on the army increased, making money almost worthless. Order was finally restored by Emperor Diocletian, a strong ruler who decided to divide imperial authority to lessen the burden of command.

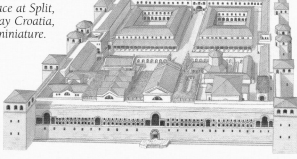

Emperor Diocletian's Palace at Split, in present-day Croatia, was a city in miniature.

THE EMPIRE DIVIDED

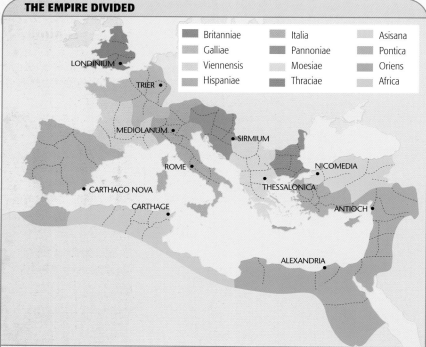

Britanniae	Italia	Asisana
Galliae	Pannoniae	Pontica
Viennensis	Moesiae	Oriens
Hispaniae	Thraciae	Africa

LONDINIUM

TRIER

MEDIOLANUM

SIRMIUM

ROME

NICOMEDIA

THESSALONICA

CARTHAGO NOVA

CARTHAGE

ANTIOCH

ALEXANDRIA

The Battle of the Milvian Bridge outside Rome, where Constantine's forces defeated Maxentius in 312 CE.

Division of Power

Each of the four tetrarchs controlled his own geographic area from four new capitals. Emperors Diocletian and Galerius controlled the East from Thessalonica and Nicomedia while emperors Maxentius and Constantius I ruled in the West from Mediolanum (present-day Milan) and Trier. As a result of Emperor Diocletian's reorganization, provinces were arranged into 12 dioceses, or administrative regimes, each ruled by a vicar. To prevent any single provincial governor or vicar from gaining too much power, governors and vicars were not given military authority. Instead, the army was controlled by a separate system independent of provincial boundaries.

The Arch of Constantine in Rome, built to commemorate the emperor's victory over his rival Maxentius.

Constantine's Victory

The weakness of the Tetrarchy was that it only worked when all four rulers agreed to co-operate. After Emperor Diocletian's reign the system broke down and rival emperors in the East and West vied for power. The man who reunited the empire was Emperor Constantine. First he overcame three rivals to become emperor in the West. He then defeated the Eastern emperor, Maximian, to become sole ruler in 324 CE. Emperor Constantine built his capital, Constantinople, on the site of the ancient city of Byzantium (present-day Istanbul).

Christianity Recognized

Emperor Constantine was won over to Christianity by a vision of the cross of Jesus Christ before his victory at the Milvian Bridge. The faith had spread widely by his day, but had been fiercely persecuted, particularly by Emperor Diocletian. Now Constantine not merely tolerated but actively encouraged Christianity, building many churches. According to some, he himself was baptised a Christian on his deathbed.

THE DECLINE

248
The 1000th anniversary of the founding of the city of Rome is celebrated with shows and games.

260–274
Postumus (reigned 260–269), governor of Lower Germany, is proclaimed emperor by the Rhine legions. A separate state, known as the Gallic Empire, survives for almost 15 years.

274
Emperor Aurelian's (reigned 270–275) attempt to increase the value of imperial currency ends in revolt.

286
Emperor Diocletian divides imperial authority.

312
Constantine defeats his rival Maxentius to become emperor.

313
Emperor Constantine ends persecution of Christians.

324
Constantinople is founded as the chief city of the Eastern Empire.

361
Emperor Julian seeks to revive paganism.

363
Pagan revival ends with death of Emperor Julian.

391
Emperor Theodosius I makes Christianity the official religion of the empire.

392
Emperor Theodosius I briefly reunites the Eastern and Western halves of the Empire.

395
The Empire is divided permanently.

Crisis in the West

In the 5th century CE, the Western Empire collapsed, although Rome's eastern provinces went on to survive as the Christian Byzantine Empire. Rome was fatally weakened when it lost control of the frontiers on the Rhine and Danube rivers that it had held for over four centuries. A wave of Germanic peoples swept into Gaul and other western provinces and also into Italy—even, on two occasions, into Rome itself. Yet all was not completely lost. These "barbarian" invaders themselves adopted some features of the Roman civilization they displaced.

Stilicho, half-Vandal and half-Roman, was imprisoned and killed after rumors that he wanted to put his son on the Eastern throne.

Foreign Invaders in Rome

Visigoths invaded northern Italy in 401 and 403, only to be turned back by Flavius Stilicho (c. 365–408), commander of the Roman forces. He was killed in 408, and no-one else proved able to stop the invaders, who sacked Rome itself in 410—the first time it had fallen to an enemy army since 390 BCE. Forty-five years later it was the turn of the Vandals, who stayed in the city for two weeks to plunder its treasures.

Ravenna

After the Visigothic invasions of northern Italy in 401 and 403 CE, Emperor Honorius (reigned 395–423 CE), son of Emperor Theodosius I (reigned 379–395 CE), decided that Rome was no longer safe from attack. Instead he moved his court to Ravenna in northeastern Italy, which was protected by lagoons. Ravenna remained the capital of the Western Empire until its fall.

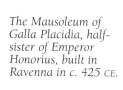

The Mausoleum of Galla Placidia, half-sister of Emperor Honorius, built in Ravenna in c. 425 CE.

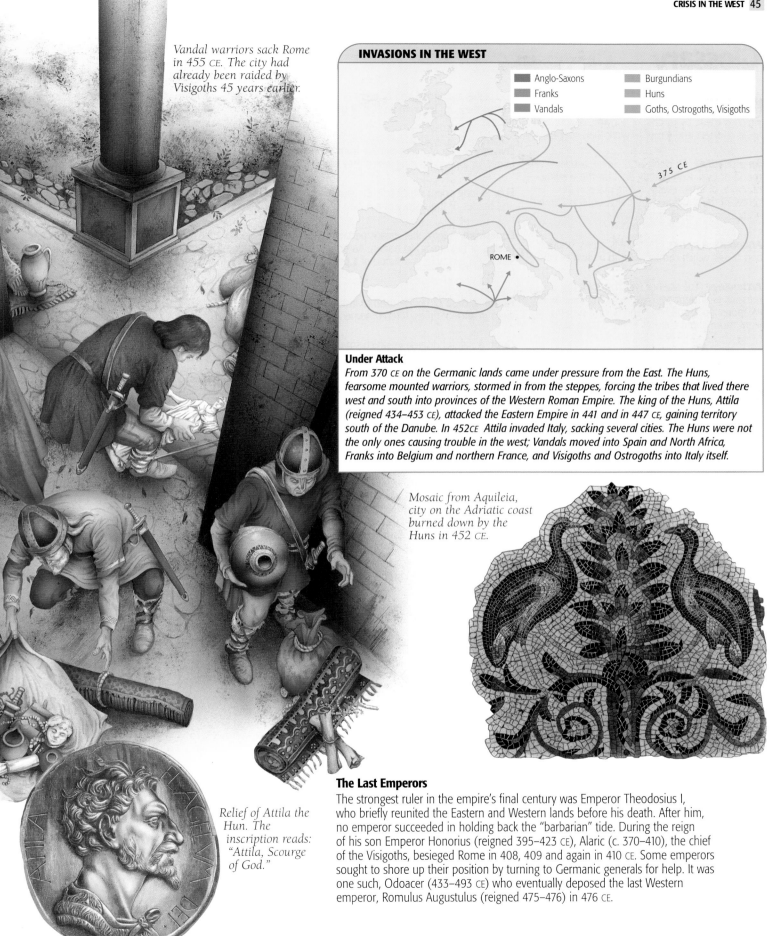

Vandal warriors sack Rome in 455 CE. The city had already been raided by Visigoths 45 years earlier.

INVASIONS IN THE WEST

- ■ Anglo-Saxons
- ■ Franks
- ■ Vandals
- ■ Burgundians
- ■ Huns
- ■ Goths, Ostrogoths, Visigoths

375 CE

ROME ●

Under Attack

From 370 CE on the Germanic lands came under pressure from the East. The Huns, fearsome mounted warriors, stormed in from the steppes, forcing the tribes that lived there west and south into provinces of the Western Roman Empire. The king of the Huns, Attila (reigned 434–453 CE), attacked the Eastern Empire in 441 and in 447 CE, gaining territory south of the Danube. In 452CE Attila invaded Italy, sacking several cities. The Huns were not the only ones causing trouble in the west; Vandals moved into Spain and North Africa, Franks into Belgium and northern France, and Visigoths and Ostrogoths into Italy itself.

Mosaic from Aquileia, city on the Adriatic coast burned down by the Huns in 452 CE.

Relief of Attila the Hun. The inscription reads: "Attila, Scourge of God."

The Last Emperors

The strongest ruler in the empire's final century was Emperor Theodosius I, who briefly reunited the Eastern and Western lands before his death. After him, no emperor succeeded in holding back the "barbarian" tide. During the reign of his son Emperor Honorius (reigned 395–423 CE), Alaric (c. 370–410), the chief of the Visigoths, besieged Rome in 408, 409 and again in 410 CE. Some emperors sought to shore up their position by turning to Germanic generals for help. It was one such, Odoacer (433–493 CE) who eventually deposed the last Western emperor, Romulus Augustulus (reigned 475–476) in 476 CE.